The Day
We Saw the Sun Come Up

by ALICE E. GOUDEY

Illustrated by

ADRIENNE

ADAMS

Charles Scribner's Sons

NEW YORK

To my husband

Printed in the United States of America
LIBRARY OF CONGRESS CATALOG CARD NUMBER 61-5787

ISBN: 0-684-12365-7

What is the sun?

The sun is a star!

Of course you know there are millions of stars. Our sun is one of them.

The sun is the star that is nearest to us.

Even though it is the nearest star it is far, far away. It is far out in space. It is ninety-three million miles away from the earth.

If you came too close to the sun you would burn up because it is very, very hot.

It is a big ball of glowing gas that gives out heat and light in all directions. It is so far away that only a small part of its heat and light reaches the earth.

The sun is larger than the moon.

It is larger than the earth. It is a million times larger than the earth. But it looks small because it is so far away.

The sun is not the largest star. Many stars are larger. But they appear to be smaller because they are farther away. Some of them appear to be tiny specks in the sky.

There are stars in the sky during the day! But we cannot see them because the sun, being closer to us, appears to be brighter.

If it were not for the sun there would be no life on earth because plants and animals need heat and light to make them grow.

One summer morning,
very, very early,
before our mother was up,
before our father was up,
before the sun was up,
my sister, Sue, and I
got up and dressed
and went outdoors.

We'd never,
in all our lives,
been up so early in the morning.
The world was very still.
It seemed as if someone
had said,
"Hush! Go quietly!
The world is not awake."
The grass was wet with dew,
and all about,
spread out on the grass,
were lacy spider webs.

We saw our cat, Christopher,
coming out across the yard,
stepping high,
and stopping to shake the dew
from each front paw
before he took another step.

We saw
the eastern sky
above the hill
all streaked with pearly-pink
just like the inside of a scallop shell.
It looked as if,
hidden behind the hill,
some great light
was glowing there.
We stood still
and watched the light grow brighter.

And then,
we saw
what we had never seen before—
a small, bright edge of sun
come up above the hill.

Without a sound,
the golden sun
was rising.
After its first bright edge
peeped up above the hill,
it kept on rising
until, at last,
we saw the whole big, round sun
hanging in the eastern sky
like a great ball
made of fire.

And now the world was filled with light.
The sun's rays shone on all the dewdrops
clinging to the lacy spider webs
and turned them into
sparkling diamonds.
Sue hopped about upon one foot
and called out to the sun.
"Good morning, Mr. Sun!"
she cried,
as if the sun could hear her.

When, at last,
we turned around,
we saw our giant shadows
stretched out dark upon the ground.
"Oh, look!"
I called to Sue.
"I stop the sun.
The sun can't shine through me!"
I held a finger up beside each ear
and made a giant shadow boy
with horns upon his head.

Sue said,
"*I* stop the sun.
The sun can't shine through *me*!"
She put her fingers together
above her head
and made a giant pixie girl
who wore a pointed cap.

When Christopher ran across the yard,
his shadow ran before him
like a giant cat.
He tried to pounce upon it.
But each time he jumped,
his shadow jumped ahead of him.

When noontime came,
the sun was high above our heads.
We could not make our giant shadows any more.
Instead,
the shadows of our bodies
lay beneath us
like small, dark pools.
And with every step we took,
they hid beneath our feet.
And then,
high above us
a small white cloud
went traveling by.
The sun
could not shine through
the little cloud,
and so
it made a shadow
on the ground.
But all around
the sun was shining.

Before we ate our lunch,
we looked for our cat, Christopher.
We called and called
and looked about us everywhere.
At last we found him
curled up in the shadow of a bush.
Christopher is very smart.
He'd found a shady place,
where the sun's warm rays
could not reach him.

When evening came,
the sun was in the western sky.
And now, again,
our giant shadows
lay upon the ground.

The sun sank lower in the sky
until, at last,
we saw it disappear
beyond the lake.
      "Goodbye, Mr. Sun!"
      Sue called.
      "Goodbye! Goodbye!"

That night,
we brushed our teeth
and put our night things on,
and then there came
the story-telling time,
the question-asking time,
the talking-time
before we went to bed.

"Once upon a time,"
our mother said,
"there was a boy,
there was a girl.
They got up early in the morning,
before their mother was up,
before their father was up,
before the sun was up,
and went outdoors.
They stood upon the earth
and watched the big, warm sun
come up in the east."

"That's us," Sue said.
"That's right," our mother said.
Sue clapped her hands.
Sue's always pleased
when she is right.
"The earth you stood on,"
our mother said,
"is like a big, round ball."
"How big is big?"
Sue asked.

Our mother said,
"If you could stand upon the highest place
and look as far as you could see,
you could never, never
see all of it at one time.
That's how big the earth is.
The land is a part of the earth.
The big oceans are a part of the earth.
Mountains and valleys,
rivers and lakes,
forests and farms and cities
are a part of the earth.
The big, round earth is all of these things."

And then our mother told us something
that seemed very strange to me.
She said,
"The big, round earth
is moving all the time.
It is turning around and around.
It is turning all day long.
It is turning all night long
while you sleep.
All the things on earth—
land and water,
farms and cities—
are riding upon the earth
as it turns and turns."
I shut my eyes and imagined
I was standing in some far-off place
looking at the big, round earth.

I imagined
it must look like this
as it turns
around and around.

I heard my mother's voice again
and came back from my far-off place.
Now she told us about the sun,
that it was shining all the time;
that it was shining
far off in the sky
even though here on earth
we might be having clouds and rain.
Then I remembered the little cloud
that went traveling by
and left its shadow on the earth,
and so, now I know
the sun cannot shine through
the clouds above
and that is why
we have our days
without sunshine.

Our mother said,
"Today,
the side of the earth you stood on
was facing the sun.
The light from the glowing sun
came down to earth
and gave you day.
Tonight,
your side of the earth
is turned away from the sun.
The light from the glowing sun
cannot shine through the earth.
You are in the shadow of the earth
and there is the darkness of night
around you."
Again, I shut my eyes and imagined
I could see the big, round earth
and the far-off sun.
I'm sure the sun,
shining on the earth,
must look like this.

The part facing the sun
is having day.
The part turned away from the sun
is having night.

I wanted to see
if this was really true,
and so I took an apple from the plate
and said to Sue,
"Let's pretend
this apple is the big, round earth
that's always turning around and around.
I'll stick two pins in it
and pretend they are us.
The flashlight that I use
to find my way about in the dark
will be the sun."

I held the apple in my hand
and let Sue hold the light.
Sue let the light shine on the pins.
"We're having day," I said.
And then I turned the apple-earth around
until the pins were in its shadow.
"And now," I said,
"we're having night
and the other side of the earth
is having day."

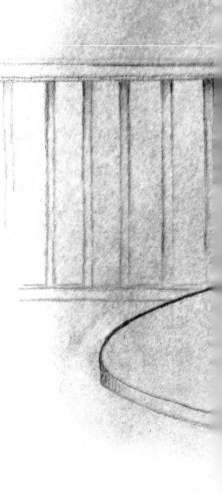

I'm glad
the earth does not stand still,
that there is an end to every night
when morning light comes back.
I'm glad
the turning of the earth
brings day
so I can see my way about.
I'm glad
the turning of the earth
brings night
so I can go to sleep
in its soft darkness.